I Know the Rules!

I FOLLOW DIRECTIONS!

By Bray Jacobson

Gareth Stevens
PUBLISHING

Please visit our website, www.garethstevens.com. For a free color catalog of all our high-quality books, call toll free 1-800-542-2595 or fax 1-877-542-2596.

Library of Congress Cataloging-in-Publication Data

Names: Jacobson, Bray, author.
Title: I follow directions! / Bray Jacobson.
Description: Buffalo, New York : Gareth Stevens Publishing, [2024] | Series: I know the rules! | Includes index.
Identifiers: LCCN 2022051524 (print) | LCCN 2022051525 (ebook) | ISBN 9781538286562 (library binding) | ISBN 9781538286555 (paperback) | ISBN 9781538286579 (ebook)
Subjects: LCSH: Cooperativeness–Juvenile literature.
Classification: LCC BJ1533.C74 J33 2024 (print) | LCC BJ1533.C74 (ebook)
  | DDC 128/.4–dc23/eng/20230104
LC record available at https://lccn.loc.gov/2022051524
LC ebook record available at https://lccn.loc.gov/2022051525

Published in 2024 by
Gareth Stevens Publishing
2544 Clinton Street
Buffalo, NY 14224

Copyright © 2024 Gareth Stevens Publishing

Designer: Claire Wrazin
Editor: Kristen Nelson

Photo credits: Cover, p. 1 R7 Photo/Shutterstock.com; p. 5 Drazen Zigic/Shutterstock.com; p. 7 BearFotos/Shutterstock.com; p. 9 Rawpixel.com/Shutterstock.com; pp. 11, 13 Maria Evseyeva/Shutterstock.com; p. 15 Ground Picture/Shutterstock.com; p. 17 candysoul/Shutterstock.com; p. 19 Monkey Business Images/Shutterstock.com; pp. 21, 23 Lopolo/Shutterstock.com; p. 24 (left) jan kranendonk/Shutterstock.com; p. 24 (right) Sergey Novikov/Shutterstock.com;

All rights reserved. No part of this book may be reproduced in any form without permission in writing from the publisher, except by a reviewer.

Printed in the United States of America

CPSIA compliance information: Batch #CSGS24: For further information contact Gareth Stevens, at 1-800-542-2595.

Contents

At School. 4

At Home 10

For Safety 14

Words to Know 24

Index. 24

I follow directions at school.
It keeps our classroom calm.

Mrs. Kent asks us to be quiet.
Margery stops talking.
She can hear the teacher.

Mr. Peabody tells us to line up.
We walk in a line.
We get to art class quickly.

I follow directions at home.
I am asked to clean my room.

I do!
I can find all my toys.

Following directions keeps us safe.

We are at the fair.
Mom tells us to stay
together.

We hold hands.
We find our way
through the crowd!

Peter falls on the playground.
A teacher tells us to move away.
We do.

Peter gets help!

Words to Know

 crowd

 line

Index

classroom, 4

clean, 10

safety, 14, 20

teacher, 6, 8, 20